DREAM AND ACTIVATE

A guide to help you realize your dreams and become successful again

By. Micheal Larry

TABLE OF CONTENT

Chapter 1: What are the Keys to Success

What is success?

The majority of individuals describe success as having a fantastic career, a lot of money, and peer esteem.

Success is the state or circumstance of satisfying a given range of expectations.

Success is the good or profitable finish of efforts or activities; the realization of one's aims.

Success can be reached when you attempt your best in all parts of whatever you do, even if it doesn't lead to significant results. If you've done your best, you should feel proud of your efforts.

Success does not come from creating abstract objectives. If you know where you're traveling, that is an accomplishment in itself, even if you don't finally reach the intended goal.

However, we all perceive success in our manner. This Is because only we alone can assess success in life and determine what it means and what gives us a feeling of achievement.

What are the primary Elements of success?

1. Socializing

socializing, the process whereby a person learns to adapt to a group and act in a way accepted by the community.

Socializing fundamentally reflects the full process of learning throughout the life cycle and is a key effect on the behavior, beliefs, and actions of adults as well as children.

What are the Benefits of Socializing

Surprisingly, mingling with people helps with the mental health of the individual.

Talking with someone may be a joyful experience, which can let you forget your troubles and become more collected and peaceful after the talk.

Social connections need to be real for them to have a favorable influence.

Socialization may provide us with a feeling of purpose by having places to go, people to see, and new things to experience.

When we have people we love who rely on us, make regular plans to interact, and continuously have something to look forward to, we are more likely to take better care of ourselves physically, intellectually, and emotionally.

2. Setting Goals.

Goal setting has a major component of an art form to it. It entails knowing yourself and your team and having a realistic grasp of everyone's capabilities.

Setting objectives is a process that varies over time. The objectives you set in your twenties will most likely be substantially different from the ones you establish in your forties.

Goal setting is the act of stating something that you want to attain and placing some particular criteria around the eventual outcome. It contains the who, what, when, where, and why.

Goals are a crucial aspect of being able to live life on purpose. They are about deliberate activity, making decisions about what you want to accomplish.

What are the Benefits of Goal setting

Goals provide you clarity on what's most important to you in life. Having objectives explains the future you want to construct for yourself with measures and timeframes.

Goals offer you direction, purpose, and objectives to attain.

Goals drive you to take action and give a clear roadmap and route to follow each day toward goal attainment.

Feedback lets you realize what you are doing properly and how you are doing. This enables you to change your expectations and your plan of action moving ahead.

3. Procrastination

We frequently imagine that projects won't take as long to do as they actually will, which may lead to a false feeling of security when we believe that we still have plenty of time to complete these duties.

Procrastination is a frequent problem, which may create different concerns, such as lost chances and increased stress.

What Is Procrastination?

Procrastination is willfully postponing a desired course of action despite anticipating to be worse off for the delay.

Ways to Avoid procrastinating

- Learning to Set tiny objectives

Oftentimes, the notion of finishing one huge chore might feel daunting. Getting from the beginning to the conclusion might seem an insurmountable endeavor. However, breaking such jobs down into many smaller parts might be advantageous.

- Learning to Remove distractions

Distractions may quickly derail your efforts, whether it's keeping your phone next to you on your desk or having the TV on in the background.

These distractions might contribute to your stress levels and encourage procrastination.

- Learning to Reward Yourself

Rewarding oneself may offer motivation to accomplish a job and help prevent procrastination.

4. Being Passionate

Being passionate involves devotion, hard effort, attention, and the determination to fail over and over again.

A passionate individual has extremely strong sentiments about something or a strong conviction in something. ... his passionate devotion to peace.

Passionate individuals are constantly focused on what can be rather than what is.

They're continually seeking their next objective with the unshakeable certainty that they'll accomplish it.

The advantages of having a passion

- It helps you to concentrate.

When you are in the appropriate mood of doing anything, you reach the flow state and you become so concentrated that you get entirely absorbed in the activity.

- Loving your principles

Just as essential as what you do is how you do it. Loving and working in harmony with your principles reveals your enthusiasm as a person.
Loving your principles also engenders the respect and dedication of others, who will regard you as a leader of integrity.

- Serving others

Use your passion to inspire others. After all, true leadership is about others, not about you. Be ready to transform your enthusiasm into an example to motivate people around you to pursue their ambitions. A real passion, like love, is infinite ... so share it.

5. Learning from Your Mistakes

Acknowledge Your Errors, Before you can learn from your errors, you have to accept full responsibility for your involvement in the result. That might be difficult occasionally, but unless you can acknowledge, "I screwed up," you aren't ready to change.

Analyze your errors, think about what caused the mistake and how you handled it, and highlight items that you performed well or badly.

Analyzing and comprehending your error might help you identify what you can do differently to guarantee that the mistake does not happen again.

It may also help you discover remedies for future problems.

Building Growth Mindset, Shame may be hard to get over, because when you're experiencing shame, you don't say to yourself, "I made a mistake", you say "I am a mistake".
This perspective inhibits you from learning and blocks solutions since we typically don't think that things can get better at that time

6. Trying another Approach.

One of the greatest methods to gain rcsults is to adjust your approach.

You can change yourself quicker than you can change other people. This provides you with amazing versatility in any scenario.

Your capacity to adjust your thinking, feeling, and acting is the key to changing your lot in life or changing the outcomes you obtain.

Chapter 2: Reduce your overall spending

One of the most efficient strategies to minimize expenditures is to limit the amount you spend on big-ticket things like housing and transportation.

But if moving to a smaller apartment or trading in for a cheaper automobile isn't doable right now or won't free up enough cash you may still drastically affect your bottom line by targeting other recurring expenditures, such as energy bills and entertainment spending.

It's vital to incorporate behavioral adjustments in your strategy to lower expenditures, too, such as setting a budget and monitoring your spending.

However, there are strategies to limit your outflow, so you may commit more money to your objectives and less to items that don't enhance your life

Ways of decreasing overall expenditure

1. Consider deferment

Some financial institutions have provided forbearance alternatives including deferral of vehicle loans during this period. If you need to, check with your bank to see what choices they may give you. While you will have to pay eventually, this might help you cut expenditures for the current period.

You should avoid deferment if you're possible, though, since you'll still accumulate interest throughout the deferral time, which eventually ends in you spending extra money.

2. Create spending categories

Everyone has a personal budget, and you may feel like there are a thousand different methods to handle yours. With the cost of living growing and everyone monitoring the pennies right now, being on top of your money is crucial. The first step to serious money management is organization.

If you want to be more in charge of your cash, categorizing your money into budget categories is a wonderful place to start.

Depending on your circumstances, spending patterns, and financial objectives, organizing your spending into personal budget categories may help you understand your spending and help you get the most from your money

Here are some of the most crucial categories and costs that your budget should include:

- Housing Expenses
- Utilities
- Transportation Clothing & Accessories
- Recreation & Lifestyle
- Medical Expenses

3. Save on interest where you can

If you have a mortgage payment or a vehicle loan, you know interest is a large percentage of your monthly payment. Whether money is tight, investigate if refinancing might help you decrease your interest payments over time.

Alternatively, if your income hasn't changed, try making an extra principal payment or two while another spending is on hold. This helps you develop equity, decreases the duration of the loan, and minimizes interest paid.

4. Eliminate impulse buying

Impulse purchasing, simply described, is buying something you didn't intend on buying.
Any spontaneous, unexpected choice to acquire goods or services is regarded to be impulse purchasing.

Many of us are familiar with this phenomenon. It happens on a trip to Target where we buy a little (or a lot more) than we intended. To add to it, we forget to get what we came for in the first place.

If you want to quit impulse purchasing once and for all, these techniques are meant to control your impulsive spending impulses;

- Plan your purchases.

- Make sure you're ready to make a significant buy.
- Take a Minute to Weigh the Cost of Impulse Purchases.
- Reevaluate what you already have.
- Reward Yourself with Free Activities Instead of Items
- Unsubscribe from emails from retail businesses.

5. Know where your money goes

One of the finest things you can do for your money is to start recording them. Being aware of where your money is going, and what it's doing, is the first step to taking charge of your finances, and putting things in order.

If you haven't been monitoring your funds, now is the time to get started.

One of the toughest things about money is understanding where you spent it. it is easy to understand your spending habits by automatically categorizing your purchases so you're always across where you're spending your cash.

When you start tracking expenses, you can separate your spending into three categories: needs, wants, and savings.

Tracking your spending regularly can give you an accurate picture of where your money is going and where you'd like it to go instead.

6. Only spend on what matters most

One may still save for and spend money on things that are connected with your own beliefs, like purchasing airfare to surprise relatives or saving money for a class one wants to attend.

By following a budget based on your beliefs, you'll feel happier and more content with your decisions, and it won't seem like a job to save money to reach objectives.

Chapter 3:Investing in various aspects of life

What Is Investing?

Investing is the act of purchasing assets that rise in value over time and produce returns in the form of income payments or capital gains.

Investing entails placing your money into something that has the potential to return a profit to you over time, increasing the amount of money you have. It often provides you with a financial interest in the firm or other asset in which you invest.

In a wider sense, an investment may also be about spending time or money to enhance your own life or the lives of others. But in the realm of finance, investment is the acquisition of stocks, real estate, and other

objects of value in the quest for capital gains or income.
One might also describe Investing as investing your money or other resources toward something you intend to make revenue, turn a profit, or provide some other beneficial benefit.

When you invest, you acquire assets that you intend to gain in value over time, which might boost your quantity of money.

The most popular kinds of investment

1. Stock

Stocks are an investment that implies you hold a stake in the firm that issued the stock. Simply, stocks are a method to grow wealth.

This is how average people invest in some of the most successful firms in the world.

For businesses, stocks are a tool to generate money to support expansion, goods, and other projects.

When you purchase the stock of a firm, you're purchasing an ownership part of that company.

A stock, often known as equity, is a security that reflects the ownership of a portion of the issuing firm.

Units of stock are termed "shares" which allows the owner to have a part of the corporation's assets and income equal to how much stock they possess.

Stocks are purchased and sold largely on stock exchanges and are the cornerstone of many individual investors' portfolios.

Stock transactions have to comply with government restrictions aimed to safeguard investors from unscrupulous tactics.

How can one make an income from stocks?

Stock investors gain money when the value of the stock they hold goes up and they're able to sell that stock for a profit. Some stocks also pay dividends, which are recurring transfers of a company's profits to investors.

2. Bonds

A bond is simply a debt an investor makes to a borrower. As with loans that you take out personally, bond investors expect to receive a full return of what was borrowed plus continuous interest payments.

Many investors appreciate bonds for the monthly income they generate via these interest payments, as well as the comparative safety they provide compared to equities.

While stock prices change day to day, highly rated bonds effectively ensure investors that they will receive payback of the amount they invested plus moderate interest.

Going back more than 90 years, investment-grade bonds as a category have not experienced a single 5- or 10-year period in which they provided negative returns.

How can investing in BONDS assist an investor?

Bonds are a fixed-income investment since investors anticipate regular income payments.

Interest is often paid to investors in regular payments, typically once or twice a year, and the complete principle is paid out at the bond's maturity date.

3. Investing in Real estate

Real estate may be a significant asset to an investing portfolio. Not only is each piece of real estate unique, but they're also not creating any more of it.

Real estate is a terrific method to boost your investment, no matter what form of real estate investing you choose.

There is a vast variety of alternatives for real estate investors, whether you want to be a highly hands-on investor or a fully hands-off one.

Real estate investment comprises the acquisition, management, and sale or leasing of real estate for profit.

Someone who actively or passively invests in real estate is termed a real estate entrepreneur or a real estate investor. Some investors actively develop, enhance or repair properties to gain more money from them.

Investing in real estate is the pinnacle of investing success from the perspective of many novice investors. Unlike stocks and bonds, real estate may be handled and stood upon regardless of market circumstances.

if you anticipate the value to rise with time. Risk varies for real estate investments. Property prices may be impacted by crime rates in a community to something as huge as the housing market collapse that led to the Great Recession.

How can investing in REAL ESTATE assist an investor?

- It gives a broad Variety of Investment Options

- Its Rental Properties Provide Passive Income

- It's Protection From Inflation
- It helps to produce Wealth & Build Equity
- It also offers a Reliable Long-term Investment

4. Mutual funds

Mutual funds enable you to combine your money with other investors to "mutually" purchase stocks, bonds, and other assets.

A mutual fund is a sort of investment vehicle where the money gathered from multiple participants is pooled together to invest in diverse assets such as bonds, equities, and/or money market investments.

Mutual funds are professionally managed by Fund Managers, who deploy the fund's assets and aim to provide returns for investors.

Benefits of mutual funds

mutual funds offer a team of specialists behind the scenes administering the mutual fund. For actively managed funds, fund managers monitor market opportunities and other techniques to select which stock, bond, and other assets to purchase and sell, to attain the investment objective of the mutual fund.

Also, mutual funds provide diversity. Since most mutual funds prefer to invest in multiple different securities, the risks associated with investing in a single investment are lessened since you're not putting all your eggs in one basket.

Why Should You Invest?

- Investing your money is vital for a few reasons. You desire to generate money to aid through times of need, job loss, or for future objectives.

- You also want to take advantage of compounding while taking into mind inflation, so your money is not worth less over time.

- In addition, if you intend on ending work at some time and retiring, investment is vital to help you attain your objectives.

Chapter 4: The common ways you can save during this journey of life.

What is Saving?

Saving is the share of income not spent on current expenses. In other words, it is the money held away for future use and not spent immediately.

Why should we save money?

Saving may be used to fulfill goals in the short term such as purchasing a mobile phone, or in the long run such as continuing to study, or else buying a vehicle or a home.

Saving money may also help us cover unforeseen expenditures, such as sickness, replacing equipment that cannot be fixed, or making an emergency trip.

Savings Can be invested and, as a consequence, you make a profit on the money you have put away. That is to say, not only will you have the dollars accessible to spend afterward, but you will also make money through the method

Sometimes the toughest part about saving money is simply getting started.

SIMPLE WAYS THAT CAN HELP YOU SAVE MONEY

- **Record your expenses**

Keeping records is the greatest approach to monitoring your income and spending. You can make better judgments for your family when you monitor the money you have and what you spend.

Once you have your data, sort the figures by categories, such as petrol, food, and mortgage, and total each sum. Use your

credit card and bank statements to make sure you've included everything.
Records also give information for income tax reasons.

It is simpler to submit your taxes if you have organized records that monitor your expenditures on tax-deductible things like medical/dental, daycare charges, and charity contributions.

- **Automate Savings Transfers**

By automating contributions into your savings account, you may simply save money without ever realizing it.

There are various methods you may establish automated savings account deposits, and each bank provides a different approach.

For example, some applications enable users to store spare change from their purchases.
Certain banks will round up purchases to the closest dollar and deposit the change in a savings account.

Other banks will offer up to 25 distinct savings accounts for all of your financial objectives.

Other programs add $1 for each debit card purchase you make to your savings account.

Automated savings systems can help you invest in yourself and your future.

- **Do it yourself**

Why pay someone when you can do it yourself for free?

If you're forking out a ton of cash for a cleaning service, it might pay off to save that money and clean your property for a time.

You could also put those youngsters to work!
By giving cleaning jobs to your kids, you may educate them about hard labor.

The experience of clearing up the home will help prepare them for when they're out of the nest.

The same counsel holds for the activities around the house, including gardening or home renovation chores.

Spend time in your yard and you'll reap various rewards. Not only will you enjoy fresh air, but you'll connect with the Earth and save money

- **Create an emergency fund.**

It's crucial to store money for a rainy day. If you confront an unexpected need, your emergency fund may assist cover the charges so that you aren't forced to dive into credit and pay interest.

Savings Goal Getter offers an Emergency Fund as one of the objectives you may select.

CONCLUSION

For one to succeed, you need to guide your steps toward the success keys, cut spending, save during this journey, and invest properly.

www.ingramcontent.com/pod-product-compliance
Lightning Source LLC
LaVergne TN
LVHW052109160826
845678LV00015B/3459

* 9 7 9 8 3 6 9 8 6 7 2 0 4 *